IRISH EMIGRATION SINCE 1921

ENDA DELANEY

Printed by
DUNDALGAN PRESS (W. Tempest) LTD.
2002

ISSN No. 0790-2913
ISBN No. 0-947 897-48-8

©
Published by
THE ECONOMIC AND SOCIAL HISTORY SOCIETY OF IRELAND

CONTENTS

INTRODUCTION

Emigration was a central feature of Irish life from the second half of the eighteenth century. Between 1801 and 1921 at least 8 million people emigrated from the island of Ireland (FITZPATRICK, 1984). From the early 1920s until the end of the twentieth century roughly 1.5 million people left independent Ireland and in excess of 500,000 people emigrated from Northern Ireland. Some of these emigrants returned. However many did not. The 1950s are etched in the popular memory as the peak of emigration from independent Ireland and, to a lesser degree, Northern Ireland. But in fact every decade witnessed significant emigration. The mid-1990s represent a remarkable turning point as, for the first time in modern Irish history, the immigration of non Irish-born people reached significant levels. In recent times, emigration has receded from public consciousness as a nation of emigrants attempts to come to terms with being a host country to immigrants. Therefore, it seems a particularly opportune time to consider the importance of emigration in the history of the two Irelands since 1921.

David Fitzpatrick's earlier study in this series (FITZPATRICK, 1984) provides an excellent synthesis of research on Irish emigration between 1801 and 1921. A similar survey of the extensive literature on emigration after 1921 has not been undertaken to date. The purpose of this essay is to assess the principal findings of this corpus of work, much of it not readily accessible since it is drawn from across a range of disciplines including economics, geography, history and sociology. The analysis is constructed around three overarching themes: the patterns and profile of the emigrant flow and how this changed over time; the causes of twentieth-century emigration; and the impact and consequences of large-scale emigration. This study adopts an explicitly comparative approach, covering both Northern Ireland and independent Ireland. It is primarily concerned with emigration from both states to other countries after 1921, and not with cross-border migration or internal migration*. For the most part, it is based on the published work of others; the names of the relevant authors

1

appear in capitals in the text, and full details may be found in the Select Bibliography. In addition, an explanation of the few technical terms used in the text (marked with an asterisk) may be found in the Glossary.

A number of colleagues and friends, each with particular fields of expertise, commented on earlier drafts of this essay and improved the accuracy and readability of the text. My thanks go to Professor Liam Kennedy, Dr Donald MacRaild, Dr Caitríona Ní Laoire and Dr Sean O'Connell. Two anonymous readers provided detailed criticisms and valuable suggestions for improvement as did the series editors, Dr Andy Bielenberg and Professor S. J. Connolly.

I

PATTERNS AND PROFILE

When I boarded the train at Listowel that morning it seemed as if everyone was leaving. It was the same at every train station along the way. Dun Laoghaire, for the first time, was a heartbreaking experience - the good-byes to husbands going back after Christmas, chubby-faced boys and girls leaving home for the first time, bewilderment written all over them, hard-faced old-stagers who never let on but who felt it the worst of all because they knew only too well what lay before them.[1]

John B. Keane's evocative description of his journey from Kerry to Great Britain in the early 1950s captures the sense of despondency that was associated with the outflow of people from Ireland for much of the period after 1921. Yet despite this perception of emigration as a national malaise, all estimates of the numbers leaving the two Irelands after 1921 are exactly that, estimates. The reason for this curious state of affairs is simple. For any state to compile precise measures of migration (either emigration or immigration), frontier controls are required to regulate, enumerate and control flows of travellers, tourists and migrants. Yet the United Kingdom and the new Irish Free State remained an integrated entity in terms of travel even after the end of the union in 1921. Except for a period between the outbreak of the Second World War and the early 1950s, no border controls existed between independent Ireland, Northern Ireland and Great Britain. Data were collected on emigration to destinations outside Europe such as Australia, Canada and the United States, and restrictions on entry to these countries also generated statistical information that facilitates some insight into the scale and significance of these flows. The other indirect estimate of the level of emigration is the number of people recorded in the census enumerations of the principal receiving societies as having been born in Ireland. However, the most reliable measures are intercensal estimates of net emigration* which provide aggregate data for a five- or ten-year period. With the growth in immigration into independent Ireland during the late 1990s, statistics of net emigration have become a less useful barometer of movement in and out of the country. Assessing the level of gross emigration* on the other hand, presents even further difficulties and for the period before the 1980s is essentially a matter for well-informed conjecture.[2] Nevertheless, there is little doubt of the sheer scale of the exodus, relative to the total population, from twentieth-century Ireland.

Table 1 Average annual rate of net emigration (per 1,000 of the average population), 1921-1991

	Independent Ireland	Northern Ireland
1921-31	-10.9	-8.0
1931-41	-3.1	-1.9
1941-51	-9.3	-3.6
1951-61	-14.1	-6.6
1961-71	-4.5	-3.8
1971-81	+4.5	-6.7
1981-91	-5.6	-4.8

Source: KENNEDY(1994), tab. 21, p. 23.

If exact numbers remain elusive, the general patterns of Irish emigration after 1921 are readily identifiable. The figures in Table 1 are based on changes in total population between censal years. After an initial peak, emigration continued at a lower rate throughout the 1920s, rising in the second half of that decade (FITZPATRICK, 1998). The international economic depression of the early 1930s dramatically reduced emigration, both north and south, as employment opportunities in the major receiving economies contracted (JOHNSON). The Second World War witnessed significant movement of Irish emigrants to Great Britain. It has been estimated that approximately 100,000 people travelled from Northern Ireland for military service and employment in Great Britain (BLAKE; ISLES and CUTHBERT). At the very least, a similar number departed for wartime work in Great Britain from independent Ireland during the Second World War, although the precise figure is the subject of some debate among historians (CONNOLLY, 2000; DELANEY, 2000).

Table 2 Estimates of emigration from independent Ireland by destination, 1988-2000 (000)

Year ending April	UK	Rest of EU	USA	Rest of world	Total
1988	40.2	2.8	7.9	10.2	61.1
1989	48.4	3.9	8.2	10.0	70.5
1990	35.8	5.1	7.7	7.6	56.2
1991	23.0	3.1	4.8	4.4	35.3
1992	16.9	7.5	3.5	5.5	33.4
1993	16.4	7.3	5.6	5.8	35.1
1994	14.8	5.5	9.6	4.9	34.8
1995	13.3	5.1	8.2	6.6	33.2
1996	14.1	5.1	5.2	6.8	31.2
1997*	12.9	4.1	4.1	7.9	29.0
1998*	8.5	4.3	4.3	4.1	21.2
1999*	10.2	4.5	5.4	8.9	29.0
2000*	6.3	4.3	3.2	8.5	22.3

* Estimated

Sources: Central Statistics Office, *Annual Population and Migration Estimates, 1988-1995* (1995); Central Statistics Office, *Population and Migration Estimates [Apr. 1998-Apr. 1999]* (1999); Central Statistics Office, *Population and Migration Estimates [Apr. 1999-Apr. 2000]* (2000).

Emigration intensified in the late 1940s and 1950s. Some indication of the extent of this outward flow is illustrated by the use of cohort depletion* techniques. GARVEY has estimated that one in every three males and females under the age of 30 years in 1946 had left independent Ireland by 1971. In the late 1950s

emigration reached levels that were reminiscent of the earlier
Famine exodus. Nearly 60,000 people left in the year 1957 alone
(see Figure 1).[3] In Northern Ireland the increase in numbers
leaving was even sharper, although the rate of movement was still
less than half that experienced by the southern state (HUGHES).
The following decade saw reduced emigration, with roughly
comparable levels north and south. In the 1970s a considerable
divergence emerged. The numbers leaving Northern Ireland rose
again, fluctuating between 10,000 and 15,000 annually
(COMPTON, 1991). In independent Ireland, for the first time in
modern Irish history, the numbers immigrating remained over a
sustained period higher than the numbers leaving. This net
inflow was due mainly to the return of Irish emigrants who had
left in the 1940s and 1950s (WALSH, 1979).

**Figure 1 Estimates of net emigration from independent Ireland,
1926-2000 (000 p.a.)**

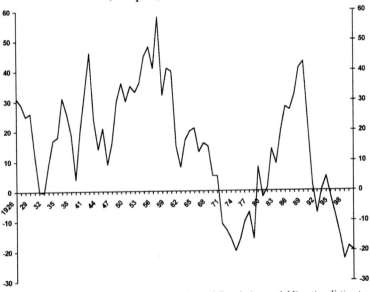

Sources: NESC; Central Statistics Office, *Annual Population and Migration Estimates,
1988-1995* (1995); Central Statistics Office, *Population and Migration Estimates [Apr.
1998-Apr. 1999]* (1999); Central Statistics Office, *Population and Migration Estimates
[Apr. 1999- Apr. 2000]* (2000).

Mass emigration again became a feature of life in the 1980s, the so-called 'new wave' of Irish emigration. In 1989, for example, the net loss of population as a result of emigration was 44,000 people, roughly 1 per cent of the total population of independent Ireland (COLEMAN). By the 1990s, on the other hand, thanks to sustained economic growth, the number of people arriving once again exceeded the numbers leaving. Yet contrary to the popular perception 'emigration' had not ceased (see Table 2). For instance, official estimates indicate that 29,000 people left in 1998-9, although nearly 47,500 people entered the country in the same period, resulting in a net inflow of 22,800.[4] Just over half of these immigrants were returned Irish emigrants, one-third were from other parts of the European Union, while the remainder came from a variety of other countries.[5] The resulting net inflow, while masking the true level of emigration, had by the late 1990s resulted in a significant increase in the total population in independent Ireland. In Northern Ireland, the net annual outflow in the 1980s was approximately 11,000 persons, leading to a slight decrease in the total population by 1991.

Where did Irish emigrants travel to in the twentieth century? From the 1930s onwards, roughly three-quarters were destined for Great Britain and one-eighth for the United States, with Canada and Australia accounting for most of the remainder (DRUDY; WALSH, 1974). North America, which had been the destination for the majority of emigrants in the previous century, declined in importance during the interwar years. This shift may be explained by reference to a combination of factors. In the first instance, legislation introduced in the United States in 1921 and 1924 aimed to reduce the level of immigration by assigning numerical quotas for each national grouping. Immigrants from independent Ireland, averaging 25,000 persons annually in the mid-1920s, decreased to just over 14,000 in 1930. From the 1930s, prospective immigrants had to demonstrate that they had substantial capital and nominate an American citizen who guaranteed to indemnify the state against the individual becoming a public charge (COMMISSION ON EMIGRATION). As in other European societies (see GEMERY), however, the principal explanation for the decline in emigration to the United States and Canada in the

1930s was not restrictive American legislation but the impact of the Wall Street Crash of 1929 and the subsequent global economic depression, producing mass unemployment in what had previously been attractive destinations for European migrants. In fact, emigration from independent Ireland to the United States, Canada and Australia virtually ceased. The numbers leaving for these destinations dropped sharply from 15,966 people in 1930 to 1,462 people in 1931 (COMMISSION ON EMIGRATION), and during the 1930s emigrants to destinations outside the British Isles, mainly the United States and Canada, averaged a mere 1,000 persons each year.[6]

Before turning to the emigrant flow to Great Britain, which looms large in the history of Irish emigration since 1921, it would be useful to outline briefly the patterns of emigration to other countries. Between 1924 and 1952 emigration to the United States accounted for four-fifths of such movement from independent Ireland, with Canada and Australia constituting 10 per cent and 5 per cent respectively (COMMISSION ON EMIGRATION). The McCarran-Walter Act of 1952 favoured northern European countries with generous quotas, which remained in place until abolished by the Immigration and Nationality Act of 1965 (LOBO and SALVO). Throughout this period Irish immigration into the United States, averaging 6,700 persons annually, remained below the quota, as was the case with most other European countries (DRUDY). It was only in the 1980s that the United States regained its popularity as a destination for Irish emigrants, many of whom entered the country illegally (CORCORAN). In the 1980s about one in seven people leaving independent Ireland travelled to the United States (NESC). The resurgence of emigration to the United States was a reflection of the employment opportunities available there and the severity of the economic recession in Great Britain (Ó GRÁDA and WALSH, 1994). Less is known about other destinations for twentieth-century Irish emigrants, such as Australia, Canada, New Zealand and South Africa. Relative to the size of the outflow to the United States, travel to Canada has remained a minor yet important element of Irish emigration, especially in the case of Northern Ireland. Between 1921 and 1930 roughly 60,000 people left Ireland for Canada (AKENSON,

1993), including former members of the Royal Irish Constabulary who were offered financial assistance to move to Canada and Australia after the force was disbanded in 1922 (FEDOROWICH, 1996, 1999). By 1961 the Irish-born population in Canada, mostly emigrants from Northern Ireland, accounted for nearly 5 per cent of the total population (AKENSON, 1993). Australia was likewise a well-trodden destination for Irish emigrants since the mid-nineteenth century and this continued to be the case in the early twentieth century. However, in the interwar years the numbers leaving Ireland for Australia declined sharply (ROSE). Emigrants from Northern Ireland destined for Canada and Australia in the 1920s and 1930s were eligible to receive government assistance under the Empire Settlement Act, 1922, although the Stormont administration, given the delicate religious demography of the province, was not anxious to promote a large-scale exodus of Protestants (FEDOROWICH, 1999; FITZPATRICK, 1998). It was only with the establishment of the Assisted Passage Scheme (1947-71), that Australia again became an attractive option. Under this scheme, which aimed to attract white settlers to Australia, emigrants were provided with assistance towards the cost of the fare, hostel accommodation on arrival, access to public housing and voting rights within six months (GRIMES). Citizens of Northern Ireland, as British subjects, paid only £10 to migrate, whereas an agreement reached with the Irish state in November 1948 limited assistance to £30 for each adult fare (MCVEIGH). The numbers leaving Northern Ireland for Australia peaked in the 1960s and over the complete duration of the scheme an annual average of almost 3,000 people travelled, although some returned at a later date. New Zealand and South Africa were also destinations for twentieth-century Irish emigrants, even if at a much lower rate than before 1921 (AKENSON, 1990, 1991).

Notwithstanding the flows to countries outside Europe, Great Britain was the principal destination for twentieth-century Irish emigrants. Great Britain had received large numbers of Irish people throughout the nineteenth and early twentieth centuries; what was new was that it now became the destination of the great majority. Identifying a particular year or sequence of consecutive years in which the Irish emigrant flow came to be more or less exclusively directed across the Irish Sea is fraught with pitfalls, given the fragmentary statistical data. Nevertheless, the available evidence suggests that the turning point came in the mid-1930s as employment opportunities in Great Britain expanded with economic recovery (DELANEY, 2000; GLYNN). During the Second World War virtually all movement was to Great Britain and this continued to be the case in the immediate postwar period. The scale of the exodus is demonstrated by the growth in the size of the Irish-born population in Great Britain which nearly doubled between 1931 and 1951 (JACKSON, 1963). From 1951 until 1971 roughly four out of every five migrants who left independent Ireland departed for Great Britain (WALSH, 1974). Since the 1970s the proportion of the flow travelling to Great Britain has declined, and it decreased even further in the late 1990s, when only a third of all migrants were destined for Great Britain.[7] Great Britain was also the principal destination for emigrants from Northern Ireland throughout the postwar period (COMPTON, 1986, 1991).

Why did Great Britain prove to be the destination of choice for so many migrants from twentieth-century Ireland and how can we explain the contrast with patterns of emigration from nineteenth-century Ireland? The first part of the explanation lies in the issue of access. Citizens of independent Ireland, except for the period of the Second World War and shortly afterwards, retained the right of free entry into the United Kingdom. Once there they could work in any sphere of employment and were entitled to the same voting and residence rights as British citizens. Emigrants from Northern Ireland were British citizens. The second element was the high demand for labour, which ensured that Irish emigrants were able to secure employment with relative ease. The importance of this point was underlined during the 1970s and early 1980s, when mass unemployment in Great Britain led to an increasing proportion of the Irish emigrant flow being again redirected towards the United States. Lastly, cheap and frequent transport links across the Irish Sea put the British labour market within easy reach of most Irish emigrants, and allowed for repeated visits home. As DALY (1999) has observed emigration was 'often punctuated by return visits and periods of employment in Ireland'.[8] Systematic analysis of cross-channel air and sea passenger movements between 1960 and 1990 underlines the tremendous expansion in transportation facilitates during this period (Ó RIAIN). In short, Great Britain proved to be the destination for so many Irish emigrants because there were no restrictions on entry, cultural similarities existed such as a common language, employment was readily available and the journey itself did not involve a large initial outlay of capital.

One significant feature of the 'new wave' of Irish emigration of the 1980s and early 1990s was the greater variety of destinations. As we have seen, Great Britain and the United States accounted for the majority of the flow. However mainland Europe also received small yet significant numbers of young Irish people, although the 'European' nature of this 'new wave' emigration has been exaggerated, as noted by MACLAUGHLIN (1994) and SHUTTLEWORTH (1997). The level of emigration to other European Union countries oscillated from nearly a quarter of the total annual outflow in 1992 to just under 5 per cent in 1988 (see Table 2). To some extent this pattern was to be expected, given the provisions for the free movement of labour within the various treaties of the European Union, especially the Single European Act of 1987, and the greater emphasis placed on European languages in Irish schools and third-level institutions from the 1980s onwards. In addition, the closer integration of the Irish and European labour markets meant that educational and other qualifications were recognised, though not always fully rewarded in terms of remuneration.

Most other European migrant flows were dominated by single males, but Ireland, north and south, differed in this key respect, following a pattern established in the nineteenth century (FITZPATRICK, 1984). For independent Ireland from 1926 until 1971 the overall sex ratio was 973 females emigrating per 1,000 males.[9] Over the longer period between 1926 and 1996 the difference between the sexes in terms of net emigration was negligible.[10] KENNEDY (1973) argued that in 'normal' circumstances, that is without a European war, a higher rate of female emigration from Ireland was the established pattern since the mid-nineteenth century and this holds true until the 1970s, with the notable exception of the mass exodus of the 1950s. From the 1970s onwards the situation is more complicated, with differences in each intercensal period. In Northern Ireland the gender differential was more marked in the postwar era, with a greater number of males emigrating than females, although by the 1980s this gap had narrowed (COMPTON, 1976, 1991). Throughout the 1990s roughly equal numbers of males and females emigrated from Northern Ireland.[11]

An overriding characteristic of the emigrant profile was the relative youth of the persons who left twentieth-century Ireland. As was the case prior to 1921, the majority were under the age of 30 years (COMPTON, 1976, 1991; NESC; Ó GRÁDA and WALSH, 1994). Between 1943 and 1951, when detailed information is available on the age of recipients of travel permits and identity cards, over 70 per cent of females were under the age of 25 years; for males almost one-half were below the age of 25 years and two-thirds were less than 30 years (COMMISSION ON EMIGRATION). Another way of illustrating the impact of emigration on the younger sections of the population is through the use of cohort depletion* techniques or survivorship ratios. To take the 1950s, an era of mass emigration, as an example, over half of those aged between 10 and 14 years in the period between 1946 and 1951 had left the country by the early 1960s (Ó GRÁDA and WALSH, 1994). Similar exercises, for both independent Ireland and Northern Ireland, yield comparable results (COMPTON, 1976; GARVEY; NESC).

Given the relative youth of the migrant flow and the late age of marriage in independent Ireland until the 1960s, it would be expected that the majority who left were single. There is no direct source of information available on the marital status of emigrants. In times of heavy emigration, such as the immediate postwar period and throughout the 1950s, it seems likely that the proportion of emigrants who were married increased. On the other hand in the 1960s, at a time of greatly reduced emigration, less than 10 per cent of the total net outflow were married (GARVEY). For married persons, leaving for Great Britain for a couple of years presented the opportunity to earn income, with the ambition of returning home to raise children at a later date. The extent of emigration also affected the level of family movement. As Ó GRÁDA and WALSH (1994) have noted, when the level of emigration rose significantly, as in the 1950s, the departure of complete families became more common. Families were also more likely to take advantage of the Assisted Passage Scheme to Australia and other forms of long-distance emigration to Canada and the United States, since such moves were conceived of as offering new lives elsewhere, rather than simply representing a temporary expedient.

Emigrants came from every county throughout Ireland. The areas that endured the highest rates of emigration over time were those along the western seaboard and north-western counties such as Leitrim and Roscommon (see Figure 2). In Northern Ireland, many emigrants came from rural areas of Armagh, Fermanagh and Tyrone, although all counties experienced out-migration, in part to other areas within Northern Ireland. Detailed statistical analysis undertaken by Ó GRÁDA and WALSH (1994) demonstrates the stability in the regional patterns of emigration over time from the 1920s until the 1970s. Counties such as Cork, Kerry, Mayo, Donegal, Longford, Leitrim and Cavan endured the most significant losses of population as a result of emigration. This apparent continuity in the regional patterns of emigration tends, however, to mask some underlying sharp changes over time. During periods of heavy emigration, the areas which historically had suffered disproportionate losses continued to do so, albeit at a higher level, as estimates of cohort depletion* demonstrate (see Figure 2). Other counties that traditionally had been only marginally affected became regions with high emigration rates, as was the experience in south Leinster during the 1940s and 1950s. Therefore no county, north or south, was left untouched by emigration, but its impact was greatest on those areas with a predominantly rural population, small farm holdings and an absence of industrial or manufacturing employment.

Changes in the distribution of the total population shaped the regional patterns of emigration. Up to the 1970s internal migration was more common in Northern Ireland, with people leaving mid-Ulster for Belfast and its hinterland, than in independent Ireland, where internal migration accounted for only a fraction of population movement (GEARY and HUGHES; HUGHES and WALSH, 1980). With the growth of employment in Dublin and the surrounding region, however, the capital city became the focus for increased numbers of internal migrants. In the 1980s, on the other hand, Dublin was an area of net emigration, in part owing to the effects of the recession on employment, but also due to the fact that the city represented a staging post for migrants from other parts of Ireland who subsequently opted to leave the country (NESC). Many emigrants in the 1980s and 1990s came from urban backgrounds, reflecting the changes in the overall distribution of the population.

The fragmentary data available underline the unskilled nature of the Irish emigrant flow after 1921. Information on emigrants from independent Ireland to places other than Great Britain in the interwar years demonstrates that two-thirds of those leaving, both male and female, listed unskilled employment as their last occupation before emigrating, though in some cases this may reflect weak aspirations rather than prior experience. In the 1940s nearly three-quarters of male applicants for travel documents were unskilled workers, and over half of females described themselves as domestic servants (COMMISSION ON EMIGRATION). In the 1950s and 1960s agricultural labourers, small farmers and their relatives made up the majority of those leaving agriculture, and in many cases the country also (WALSH, 1969, 1971). Other more diverse sources confirm that unskilled emigrants predominated in the exodus from Ireland during the first half of the twentieth century (DELANEY, 2000), as they had in the previous century. Needless to say, the standard designation of small farmers and other agricultural workers as 'unskilled' merely meant that the skills that they had were irrelevant to an urban industrial setting. Notwithstanding the lack of systematic analysis of the emigrant profile in terms of class origins, it seems reasonable to assume that it was young people in the lower middle class and the working class, both in rural and urban areas, who were most likely to emigrate. The economic recessions impacted hardest on these groupings and this together with the limited opportunities for social mobility within twentieth-century Ireland made emigration attractive.

Figure 2 Cohort Depletion, 1926-1971*

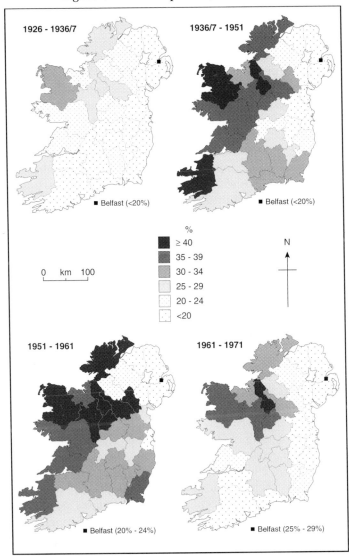

*Cohort depletion is the percentage of the cohort aged 5-24 years who had 'disappeared' in the following census. This measure makes no adjustment for internal migration or mortality.

The traditional picture of the twentieth-century emigrant flow as composed of a homogenous mass of unskilled workers from rural Ireland nevertheless requires some qualification. There is evidence that those with skills and qualifications did leave prior to the 1960s, a phenomenon contemporaries labelled the 'brain drain'. It has been suggested that over two-thirds of those who had graduated from medical schools in independent Ireland after 1950 had emigrated by 1966 (GISH). The Commission on Higher Education in 1967 suggested a much lower figure of 25 per cent, but this related 'only to those who might voluntarily emigrate, as distinct from graduates who might be obliged to do so owing to lack of employment opportunities at home'.[12] Notwithstanding the obvious problems with such an arbitrary distinction, it is clear that a long-established tradition of graduate emigration did exist after 1921, and was not solely confined to doctors (LYNN). It has been argued by HANLON (1997) that the actual proportion of skilled migrants leaving independent Ireland fluctuated between 10 per cent and 25 per cent, but definitive information on this aspect of the outflow is not available prior to the 1980s.

From the 1980s onwards, graduate emigration attracted greater scholarly interest and public comment (see SHUTTLE-WORTH, 1991, 1997). To some extent, the growth in graduate emigration was to be anticipated, given the expansion in second and third-level education from the 1960s, since the emigrant flow will mirror the overall educational profile of the total population. The graduate exodus also reflected the opportunities created by the demand for skilled workers, not just in Great Britain but also in mainland Europe, and the United States, which young middle-class Irish emigrants were well equipped to respond to. One finding of particular interest, from the 1980s onwards, is that emigrants from Northern Ireland living in Great Britain had higher levels of educational achievement that those from independent Ireland, reflecting the earlier moves north of the border towards the widening of access to secondary and third-level education (BREEN, HEATH and WHELAN).

Estimating the differential impact of emigration on religious denominations is a complex procedure. In more recent times, these difficulties are compounded by refusals, particularly in

Northern Ireland, to answer questions on religion, by growing numbers claiming to be of 'no religion' in census enumerations, and by transfers between religious groupings. Nevertheless, it is possible, using cohort depletion* techniques, to examine in an approximate fashion the rate of emigration differentiated by religious grouping. In the interwar years and during the Second World War, Protestants emigrated from independent Ireland at a higher rate than Catholics, but in the postwar period, up to 1961, the rate for Catholics was somewhat higher (SEXTON and O'LEARY; WALSH, 1970, 1975). The emigration of Protestants prior to the Second World War also reflected class and educational differences. As KENNEDY (1973) has shown the Protestants who left independent Ireland in the 1920s and 1930s were likely to have better education and more marketable skills. In the 1960s the differences in the impact of emigration on the various religious denominations lessened. Catholics emigrated at much the same rate as other religious groupings and this continued to be the case into the 1990s (SEXTON AND O'LEARY). In Northern Ireland the failure of the traditionally higher birth rate among Catholics to produce a substantial rise in the Catholic share of total population is generally explained by the higher level of Catholic emigration up to the 1960s (WALSH, 1970). Nearly 60 per cent of emigrants from Northern Ireland between 1939 and 1951 were Catholics, even though Catholics accounted for only one-third of the total population.[13] In the next ten years almost two-thirds of emigrants were Catholics (COMPTON, 1976). However, in the 1960s the differences narrowed somewhat and throughout the 1970s and 1980s Protestants emigrated from Northern Ireland at a higher rate than Catholics (Ó GRÁDA and WALSH, 1995). The significance of these differences is that the rate of emigration directly affected the religious composition of the population, which in Northern Ireland had obvious constitutional implications. In the south, the level of emigration contributed to the long-term decline of the Protestant community.

Traditionally inflows of immigrants into independent Ireland and Northern Ireland were overshadowed by the numbers actually leaving and only from the 1980s onwards is detailed information available on gross inflows and outflows. In the early 1930s as a result of the impact of the global economic crisis the numbers coming back to the Irish Free State exceeded those departing for other countries (see Figure 1). Similarly, the outbreak of the Second World War in 1939 prompted a significant return flow from Great Britain, reflecting a fear of possible conscription to serve into the armed forces and a preference for life in a neutral country. Throughout the postwar period there is evidence suggesting frequent movement across the Irish Sea in both directions, influenced by conditions at home and in Great Britain as well as by stages in individual life cycles. For instance, in the 1960s the loss as a result of emigration of 183,000 people was offset to a limited degree by a gain of over 50,000 people born outside the Irish state, mainly the offspring of emigrants.[14] The 1970s, as we observed earlier, witnessed a significant reversal in Irish demographic history as the numbers immigrating into independent Ireland exceeded those leaving. This was not the onset of large-scale immigration but rather the return of Irish emigrants from Great Britain, the United States and elsewhere as a result of the more prosperous state of the economy. This return flow included a large number of married persons with children who had been born abroad, as was the case in the 1960s (GARVEY; J. A. WALSH). In the 1980s and 1990s immigration averaged over 30,000 persons per annum, although the number of people coming to independent Ireland rose further in the 1990s (COURTNEY). Even though the majority of immigrants throughout the 1990s were Irish-born, the attractions of rapid economic growth ensured that immigration from other EU countries and non-EU countries increased over time. This generated much public controversy about refugees and asylum-seekers arriving in independent Ireland, notwithstanding the relatively small numbers involved. For Northern Ireland the annual gross inflow between 1975 and 1990 fluctuated between 6,000 and 10,000 persons (COMPTON, 1991).

Generalisations therefore fail to capture the complexity of the patterns of Irish emigration after 1921. Emigration reached its peak in the 1950s and 1980s. Great Britain replaced the United States as the principal destination for Irish emigrants in the 1930s.

Throughout the 1980s and early 1990s young Irish people opted for a wider variety of destinations. In part these patterns have been shaped by the demand for labour in other economies. The profile of the Irish emigrant flow in terms of skills and educational background has also changed over time. In the 1930s the typical emigrant was from the ranks of the labouring or lower middle classes and from an agricultural background, with few marketable skills for the industrial economy to which he or she invariably went. By the late 1990s emigrants were more likely to be from the enlarged ranks of the middle class. At very least they would usually have completed secondary education, and a significant minority were graduates. These changes in the emigrant profile mirrored wider developments in twentieth-century Irish society as a whole.

II

CAUSES

While the fundamental cause of emigration is economic, in most cases the decision to emigrate cannot be ascribed to any single motive but to the interplay of a number of motives . . . It is not possible, therefore, to attribute emigration to a single cause which would account satisfactorily for the decision to emigrate in all cases.[15]

The Commission on Emigration and Other Population Problems, established by the inter-party government in 1948, rightly emphasised the multiplicity of factors involved in the origins and perpetuation of emigration from Ireland since 1921. Traditionally scholars have explained migration, both internal and international movement, in terms of 'push-pull' models. Under this formulation, migrants were 'pushed' from their homeland by a range of factors including population pressure, a lack of employment or a scarcity of opportunities to own or hold land. The 'pull', or attraction of other societies, existed in the form of a perceived abundance of jobs and land. In recent times, historians and social scientists have recognised that migration is a much more multifaceted and dynamic process than this simplistic model suggests. Detailed biographical life histories such as NÍ LAOIRE's research on the migration of young people from North Cork in the 1980s and 1990s point to the complexities involved in the decision to leave. The tendency to view this phenomenon as resulting exclusively from economic causes has also been tempered by an appreciation of the social processes associated with migration, for example, its organisation through flows of information between migrants and prospective migrants (MASSEY ET AL). Equally it is now commonly acknowledged that the process of migration involves structural changes in both the sending and receiving societies. In other words, a real understanding of the causes and determinants of migration always requires an examination of conditions in two or more regions or countries.

Explanations of mass emigration from twentieth-century Ireland have tended to vary with the strictly demarcated boundaries of academic disciplines. Economists invariably stress wage differentials* and the rate of unemployment, whereas sociologists focus on social structure and on such typical features of a migration-prone society as well-established migrant networks*. Some geographers such as MACLAUGHLIN (1994) argue that modern Irish emigration should be assessed within world-systems theory: or in other words, that the exodus illustrates not only the marginal location of Ireland within the world economy, but also its peripheral status. Some debate also exists about the appropriate unit of analysis. On the one hand, there is the view that mass emigration is the result of individual decisions, after a rational calculation of the 'costs' and 'benefits' of staying or leaving. Recent research by GUINNANE, on the other hand, underlines the extent to which the timing of any decision to leave home was shaped by the economic needs of the household. For their part, historians have tended to draw rather eclectically from this varied body of theory. For the purposes of clarity the discussion that follows groups the causes of emigration under two broad headings. First, there are structural aspects of Irish economy and society, such as the performance of the economy, or changes in the composition of the labour force. Secondly, there are social and cultural factors, including the development of elaborate migrant networks* or the departure of members of minority religious groupings in response to perceived discrimination on the basis of religion. Needless to say no single all-encompassing explanation captures the dynamics of Irish emigration since 1921 and, as will be seen, the relationship between these causes differed over time and geographical location.

Table 3 Employment in Ireland by sector, 1930-1990 (%)

	Agriculture			Industry			Services		
	1930	1960	1990	1930	1960	1990	1930	1960	1990
Independent Ireland	48	37	15	15	24	29	37	39	55
Northern Ireland	26	14	10	37	41	33	37	45	57

Source: After Ó GRÁDA (1997), tab. 6.1, p. 168. The data for Northern Ireland relate to 1926, 1961 and 1993.

One of the principal causes of emigration is the changes in the wider economic and social environment. In the case of independent Ireland, an obvious explanation relates to the structure of the labour force (see Table 3). In 1926 over half of the economically active population were employed in agriculture, but by the 1990s this had fallen to just over one in ten (Ó GRÁDA, 1994, 1997). As KENNEDY (1973) has observed, the impact of technology reduced the demand for farm labour, aided in part by rapid progress of the rural electrification scheme. Tractors, milking machines and other labour saving devices were widely adopted on holdings throughout the postwar period. For example, during the 1950s the number of tractors increased by 350 per cent.[16] The willingness to adopt new techniques was driven for the most part by the desire to raise the level of productivity and offset the obvious drudgery of the more routine elements of farm work. Even though at first only larger farmers could afford the initial outlay of capital involved to purchase tractors and milking machines, over time agriculture became a less labour intensive form of economic activity and the decline in tillage farms in the west of Ireland accelerated this process. This directly determined the level of emigration owing to the contraction in the opportunities available in agriculture compounded by the shortage of alternative employment in the manufacturing or industrial sectors. Emigration therefore became a realistic (and realisable) route by which to secure employment, albeit in a different environment. The decreased demand for labour concerned not only farmers and labourers, but also relatives assisting on the farm. This broad grouping, which had accounted for a third of the agricultural labour force in independent Ireland in 1951, had roughly halved by 1971.[17]

The nature of agricultural production also determined the level of demand for labour until the 1960s. In the 1920s the agricultural economy was orientated towards the export of pastoral products to Great Britain. The economic policy of the Cumann na nGaedheal government centred on the ability to export agricultural products at competitive prices. Opposition politicians such as Eamon de Valera argued that this was promoting not solely the export of agricultural products, but also the export of Irish citizens (JOHNSON, 1985). Fianna Fáil administrations in the 1930s and 1940s attempted to reverse earlier trends by reorienting agriculture around labour intensive tillage on small family holdings, but this goal proved to be illusory.

Closely associated with the decrease in the demand for agricultural employment was the gradual process whereby the number of small farm holdings declined over the course of the twentieth century. Smaller, uneconomic units which were located in the poorer areas of western and north-western Ireland were simply unable to provide what was perceived to be an 'acceptable' standard of living. Agriculture compared unfavourably with the better prospects afforded by other forms of employment. The reduction in the number of small farms reflects not only a move towards modernisation of agriculture, but an accompanying decrease in the total agricultural population. This process was not unique to Ireland; precarious rural economies based on small, uneconomic holdings and outdated technology collapsed throughout twentieth-century Europe, leading to the displacement of large numbers of people from agriculture. Northern Portugal and southern Italy provide particularly stark examples of this general pattern.

A constant assertion in much of the contemporary discussion of emigration from twentieth-century Ireland was that the number of people leaving was directly associated with the level of industrial development. To a large degree, this emphasis on the relationship between Irish economic growth and emigration was close to the mark. Given adequate industrial growth and the concomitant employment creation, the changes in agriculture would simply have resulted in a redistribution of employment across a number of sectors of the labour force. As it was the limited development, until the 1960s, of the industrial and service sectors of the Irish economy ensured that non-agricultural employment was difficult to obtain. As was the case in the nineteenth and early twentieth centuries, the decision to move from agricultural to industrial employment in many cases involved leaving Ireland for Great Britain or North America.

The absence of sustained economic development, generating sufficient employment opportunities to alleviate the need to travel to Great Britain or elsewhere, was starkly illustrated by a plethora of rural surveys conducted in the postwar period. In east Limerick, west Cork, Sligo, Mayo and other parts of Ireland the conclusion was the same: the creation of non-agricultural employment, allowing young people to obtain secure and reasonably well-paid jobs, would reduce the level of emigration (DELANEY, 2000). It should be noted that the economic policies of various governments recognised the need to foster non-agricultural employment to offset the effects of the displacement of people from agriculture. Nevertheless, much emphasis was placed on serving the domestic market, as was the case with the protectionist policy that Fianna Fáil pursued with some vigour in the 1930s. In the short-term the drive to create manufacturing industries behind protective walls resulted in a substantial increase in industrial employment, but the benefits of this policy were short-lived (Ó GRÁDA, 1997). Policy-makers across the political spectrum understood that to reduce the extent of emigration, substantial additional employment was needed. For example, an official statement of Irish government policy stated in 1960 that the 'policy of the Irish government is to remove the economic need for emigration by promoting increased economic activity at home'.[18] From the mid-1960s onwards the benefits of an export-orientated economic policy, based in large part on attracting foreign investment, were reflected in increased employment in the industrial and service sectors (see Table 3). However the uncertain foundations of this policy were exposed in the economic crises of the 1980s.

A central question relating to the range of factors that determined the level of emigration from twentieth-century Ireland is the extent to which this exodus was driven by economic necessity. As we have seen, in general until the mid-1990s the economic situation did not hold out an attractive future for young people, except those in well-paid steady employment, and there is thus little doubt that for some emigration was a flight from dire poverty. But was this an exodus from the endemic poverty that is so graphically described in MCCOURT'S autobiographical account of life in Limerick in the 1930s and early 1940s? There is no doubt that many people existed in grinding poverty until the

1960s. For example, an unpublished study of Cork city during the Second World War found that 45 per cent of households were living below the poverty line.[19] Such conditions, in both urban and rural areas, were undoubtedly a driving force behind Irish emigration after 1921. Donall MAC AMHLAIGH, who left in the early 1950s, records his bitterness at having been forced by economic necessity to leave his native land to work in Great Britain. However emigration can also be viewed as an outcome of socio-cultural change. From the Second World War onwards, in particular, emigrants left not solely out of economic necessity, but because they aspired towards a higher standard of living.

The clearest example of this is the evidence that in many cases it was not restrictive inheritance patterns that drove people out, but a rejection of farm life. The relationship between household structure, inheritance and emigration in post-Famine Ireland is, according to conventional logic, a direct one, neatly illustrated in the adage: 'One for the farm, the rest for the road'.[20] Studies by GUINNANE, KENNEDY (1991) and Ó GRÁDA (1980), however, suggest more complex sets of inheritance patterns than the simple transfer to the eldest son; some heirs looked upon the transfer of the family holding as a distinct disadvantage, especially when compared with the brighter (and more secure) futures which beckoned abroad. By the postwar period agriculture as a livelihood was far less attractive to those in search of economic security. A survey of emigration from Co. Mayo conducted in 1948 for the purposes of the Commission on Emigration and Other Population Problems, 1948-54, observed that it was not uncommon for children to stay abroad in Great Britain or the United States rather than return to take over the family holding.[21] Another study completed in the late 1960s found that a significant number of holdings in the west of Ireland had no prospective heir, and the situation was particularly acute in the case of smaller farms (SCULLY). In these cases emigration was increasingly viewed by many young people not as a necessity but as the preferred route to economic well-being.

Research undertaken by sociologists such as HANNAN (1972, 1979, 1982) has charted the process by which new values and value-systems in Irish rural communities gradually replaced traditional assumptions and norms in the postwar period. The values of the urban middle class, with an emphasis on consumption and aspirations towards a higher standard of living, became increasingly apparent in Irish rural communities. Meanwhile frequent contact with emigrant relatives encouraged greater awareness of the stark contrasts between Ireland and Great Britain in terms of living standards and lifestyles. It is argued that the emphasis placed on the welfare of the household also diminished as individual achievement became paramount, encouraging emigration as one of the principal routes to individual success. DALY (1981) has observed that the mass emigration of young women in the postwar period was evidence that 'they were placing their personal interest above those of family and society'.[22] Equally significant, detailed analysis of fragmentary survey data on motives drawn from throughout the postwar period demonstrates that emigrants frequently cited the better wages and higher standard of living available in Great Britain as the key determinant in their decision to emigrate (DELANEY, 2000). The most comprehensive study of twentieth-century Irish migration, examining over 500 young people from Co. Cavan in the mid-1960s (HANNAN, 1969, 1970), underlined the crucial significance of income and career goals in the minds of these prospective emigrants. Young people perceived that these aspirations could rarely be realised in the local community because of the scarcity of suitable employment. Education fuelled such ambitions.

For most twentieth-century emigrants the British labour market was viewed with comparative reference to conditions at home. Migrant networks* ensured that information concerning wage levels and employment opportunities were available to emigrants, thereby reducing the risks involved in the process of emigration. What emerges is that Irish emigrants were operating in the context of two closely integrated labour markets. Wage levels in specific sectors of employment such as construction and engineering were higher in Dublin than in London (O'ROURKE, 1994). But a comparison between agricultural wages in Ireland and industrial wages in Great Britain (Ó GRÁDA AND WALSH, 1994) demonstrates clearly that wage differentials* provided the incentive to migrate, although levels did converge in the 1980s and 1990s (see also WALSH, 1994). The strong demand for labour in Great Britain in the postwar decades provided the requisite security for this potentially risky move. Between the end of the Second World War and the 1970s few Irish emigrants would have experienced insurmountable difficulty in obtaining jobs in industrial, manufacturing or service employment across the Irish Sea. Given the level of knowledge about employment conditions in Great Britain (and the ease of return), prospective emigrants were simply assessing their position when faced with two possible scenarios. The first involved staying at home, and attempting to obtain scarce non-agricultural employment, which in itself probably involved moving away from the local community. The second centred on travelling to Great Britain, and seeking out a job in a factory or in the rapidly-expanding service sector with valuable information derived from friends and relatives, in the knowledge that rates of remuneration were high and return home an inexpensive option. For many, emigration thus made sound economic sense.

Was emigration a way of escaping the rigid social hierarchy of twentieth-century Ireland? Without doubt, for the sons and daughters of the rural poor, such as farm labourers and other unskilled workers, leaving Ireland provided an opportunity to circumvent the position ascribed to them solely by virtue of their father's occupation. Thus the parent of one emigrant in east Limerick in the late 1950s observed that 'one can get a job on one's merits in England. Employers don't ask who you are, but what you can do.'[23] Moreover, the veil of anonymity offered by life in industrial Britain compared favourably with the fixed and often pejorative labels of rural and small town Ireland.

The stage at which emigration occurred was determined not alone by individuals, but also by the needs of households. For instance, young people rarely emigrated before the age of 16 years, since education and the demands of the household for labour ruled out this possibility. The late teens and early twenties was the crucial stage in the life cycle. For males, the needs of the household influenced the eventual outcome. If a young male could add to the household income through employment or unpaid labour, as was the case with relatives assisting on farms, the likelihood of emigration was reduced. However, if no employment could be found and the household was unable to support another adult the imperative for emigration was strengthened, especially since remittances provided a much-needed source of income that was independent of the local economy. For young single females, who tended to stay in education slightly longer than males, the teens were equally significant in terms of emigration. The level of female employment remained relatively static in independent Ireland until the 1960s, when females began to benefit from the expansion in clerical and other jobs (DALY, 1997). In rural Ireland in particular, emigration was thus the only avenue to secure income both for the individual and, again through remittances, for the household. The emigration or dispersal of 'surplus' children, as observed by ARENSBERG and KIMBALL in their famous study of Clare in the 1930s, was essential for the well-being of the household. DALY (1999) has argued that increasingly throughout the postwar period parents could not rely on remittances from children living abroad, as economic independence and personal consumption became of far greater significance, reflecting changes in social mores. However this contention remains to be established on the basis of a wide range of evidence. The second stage, for males, at which emigration was likely to occur was after marriage, when emigration to Great Britain could be the central element of a short-term strategy to boost the income of the fledgling household and support children. In the later years of life, for both males and females, emigration was rare and usually determined by quite specific circumstances such as some economic misfortune.

Why did Ireland differ from other European countries in sending out roughly equal numbers of men and women? The explanation lies in two quite distinct aspects of the history of Irish emigration since 1921. The first relates to the increasingly circumscribed economic role of females over the last century, as limited economic opportunities were exacerbated by ideological factors such as the ubiquitous image of the woman in the household, enshrined in law in the Irish constitution of 1937. In practice, this was reflected in areas such as the bar on the employment of

married women in the civil service introduced in the 1920s and
the limited creation of female employment in the postwar period
(DALY, 1997; TRAVERS, 1995). In rural areas, the lack of female
employment was particularly acute. HANNAN (1973) has posited
that the reason for the parity in respect of gender lies in the fact
that most emigrants until the 1960s came from an agricultural
background and 'fewer women than men remain on the farm
upon completing their education'.[24] The other factor that
explains the mass emigration of Irish women was the nature of
the demand for labour in Great Britain in the twentieth century.
During the Second World War thousands of young Irish women
travelled to Great Britain to take up employment in munitions
and other industries, and in service sector occupations such as
nursing or domestic service (DELANEY, 2000, 2001). Throughout
the 1940s and 1950s the demand generated by the postwar British
economy continued to attract female emigrants, with steady
secure employment, disposable income and a life less encum-
bered by the restraints of a traditional society. One emigrant
captured the differences between living in Great Britain and life
at home in rural Ireland, remarking candidly in 1948 that she had
'[a] better life in Croydon, than in Sligo'.[25]

Conventional logic would seem to suggest that all other things
being equal these factors should have resulted in more females
leaving than males. How then can the relative parity in terms of
gender be explained? Alas, there is no simple answer to this
conundrum. As yet historians have not adequately explained why
more females did not leave and attention has been devoted to
assessing why so many women emigrated in the first place (see
DELANEY, 2001). Constraints on the level of emigration from
independent Ireland existed during the Second World War when
only those aged over 22 years were allowed to travel to Great
Britain for employment and whilst this may have adversely
affected females, who tended to leave at an earlier age, these
regulations were not strictly adhered to by officials (DELANEY,
2000). In addition, the unpaid and unenviable role of single
females in households who cared for elderly parents or
unmarried brothers ensured that, for some women at least,
familial obligations acted as a barrier to movement.

Uprooting from home and a local community for a new life elsewhere, either for a few months or for a longer duration, was undoubtedly a traumatic event in the life cycle of young Irish people. Yet few people set out to leave the known for the unknown. Instead, most scholars recognise that the process of migration proceeds in waves, with the 'pioneers' first charting the potential and possibilities of the new receiving society, to be followed in due course by other waves of migrants. The very existence of Irish communities in Great Britain, North America and Australia lessened the inherent risks involved in such a move and this explains the well-established emigrant pathways developed over the course of the twentieth century. In the case of Great Britain the Second World War proved to be an important phase, since the emigrants who left at this time created the migrant networks* which facilitated the mass emigration of the 1940s and 1950s. Such networks ensured that migrants were provided with practical help on first coming over in terms of employment and accommodation, but also determined the initial place of settlement. Contemporary surveys undertaken in the postwar period confirm the role of family members and friends in thus reducing the uncertainty involved in the process of emigration (DELANEY, 2000). In this way, migrant networks linked both societies and became embedded as a pivotal element of the social structure of not only the sending region but also migrant communities in the new societies.

Emigration was also the result of less quantifiable factors such as a sense of alienation from the dominant cultural or confessional ethos. This applies with particular force to Protestants in the Irish Free State and Catholics in Northern Ireland until the early 1970s. In independent Ireland the overarching drive in the 1920s and 1930s was to establish an Irish Catholic nationalist ethos in terms of cultural production, education and the general intellectual atmosphere. The sectarian tension that culminated in attacks on Protestants in the period between 1917 and 1923 loomed large in the minds of southern Protestants (HART, 1996, 1998). This contributed to an already established pattern of emigration among southern Protestants after 1921 (BOWEN). From 1911 until 1926 over 100,000 Protestants left what was to constitute the

Irish Free State in 1921/2. While a substantial element of this outflow was related to the end of British rule in 1922, it is estimated that roughly 60,000 were not crown officials or serving in the police or military (SEXTON AND O'LEARY). Similarly, hostile cultural pressures in Northern Ireland, where the exclusivist Ulster Unionist ethos permeated all aspects of life under state control after partition, may have convinced some northern nationalists that a brighter future lay elsewhere, especially in the wake of sectarian expulsions from places of employment between 1920 and 1922. Cultural motives for emigration may have co-existed with economic concerns. The well-charted self-imposed 'exile' of writers such as Edna O'Brien, in response to the more draconian effects of a monolithic Catholic conservatism, is another example of the relationship between dominant cultures and the emigration of ethnic, religious and intellectual minorities (DUFFY). The social authority of the Catholic Church in independent Ireland also resulted in unmarried mothers, particularly in the 1940s and 1950s, leaving on a temporary basis to give birth to children who were subsequently offered for adoption in Great Britain (GARRETT). Similarly, the availability of legal abortion in Great Britain from 1967 onwards generated a small but constant stream of women seeking to avail of services that were not available in Ireland, north or south.

Arbitrary distinctions between 'permanent' and 'temporary' migration are not helpful. Few emigrants conceived their plans in such a formulaic way. Many people leaving Ireland for Great Britain after 1921 viewed their stay as little more than a temporary expedient until conditions improved at home: the exodus during the Second World War is a striking example of this temporary movement in response to dismal economic conditions at home and abundant opportunities in Great Britain. Inexpensive transportation across the Irish Sea by sea, and later by air, facilitated frequent return visits; consequently the perception that you were never far away from home was all-pervasive and reassuring. The minority who departed to North America or Australia more clearly sought a new life elsewhere. But from the 1960s onwards the expansion of air travel placed even Sydney and San Francisco within relatively easy reach for most Irish families. The high level of movement in and out of the Irish state suggests a constant traffic of emigrants back and forth across the Irish Sea: for example in 1949 there were nearly 2.5 million journeys into independent Ireland and roughly the same outward, and this increased greatly over time.[26]

Irish emigration after 1921 is therefore the result of the interaction of a multiplicity of economic, social and cultural causes, whose relative importance varied over time and space. Leaving Ireland was a deeply-embedded feature of life prior to 1921 and emigration continued to retain its centrality for at least the next seventy years. The overarching explanation for the scale of the exodus was the failure of the Irish economy to generate sufficient employment in industry, manufacturing or services. Nevertheless, even in the unlikely event of such large-scale employment creation, it seems that some people would still have departed to fulfil income and career aspirations. When the economic situation appeared particularly bleak, as in the 1950s and 1980s, the level of emigration increased sharply. As more people left and emigration became widespread, networks ensured that the risks and uncertainty involved were lessened, thereby perpetuating the movement over time. In many respects, emigration evolved as a self-reproducing practice. Only with the rapid economic growth that developed in the mid-1990s did staying at home become a realistic option for an entire generation coming of age in independent Ireland.

III

IMPACT AND CONSEQUENCES

Nothing in recent centuries is so puzzling or so challenging as the strange phenomenon being enacted before our eyes: the fading away of the once great and populous nation of Ireland. If the past century's rate of decline continues for another century, the Irish will virtually disappear as a nation and will be found only as an enervated remnant in a land occupied by foreigners . . . Today Ireland is teetering perilously on the brink of near extinction as the habits of the past century persist.[27]

Emigration has been the subject of recurrent political debate in independent Ireland with the numbers leaving often considered as a crucial test of economic performance. It has been viewed as damaging to national morale, as a damning indictment of the economic policy of successive governments and, in some extreme cases, as hard evidence of the failure of independent Ireland. In reality emigration was never a wholly reliable test of economic policy, since the number of people leaving twentieth-century Ireland was in part influenced by exogenous events, such as the demand for labour in the receiving societies or the state of the international economy. But detailed analysis of the politics of Irish emigration over the period from 1921 until 1971 demonstrates that large-scale emigration was more often than not discussed in the broader context of the success or failure of the economic policy of particular administrations (DELANEY, 1998, 2000). The 1980s, likewise, are commonly associated with recession, unemployment and emigration and the failure of the Irish body politic to formulate policies that addressed these related problems. From the mid-1990s, with prosperity driven by a quite remarkable rate of economic growth, the agenda changed. The issue was no longer the numbers departing for other countries, but the level of immigration and whether this was the inevitable consequence of economic success.

It is of interest that during the revolutionary period between 1919 and 1923 the Irish Republican Army and its associated civil arm, the ministry elected by the first Dáil, attempted to control emigration (FITZPATRICK, 1996). From July 1920 the written sanction of the revolutionary government was required by all wishing to leave, and the ban on emigration was lifted by the new government only in October 1923. How rigorously these regulations were enforced is another matter (FEDOROWICH, 1999). In this case the prohibition of emigration was viewed as a means of protecting recruitment to the ranks of nationalist organisations, since it was perceived that the British authorities were encouraging young people to leave Ireland. In the 1920s and 1930s nationalist politicians continued to pay lip service to the notion of emigration as an evil, but in practice both the Cumann na nGaedheal administration and its Fianna Fáil successors pursued a policy of the free movement of labour. In 1937 Eamon de Valera outlined the principles underpinning the policy of the independent Irish state on emigration.

> The aim of the Irish government is not to provide facilities for the emigration of our people to the states of the British Commonwealth or elsewhere. Its aim is to concentrate on utilising the resources of this country and so improving the conditions of life here that our people will not have to emigrate, but will be able to find a livelihood in our country.[28]

The outbreak of the Second World War in 1939 resulted in the imposition of controls on movement across the Irish Sea, in part as a response to measures introduced by the British authorities and also with a view to protecting the home labour supply. Restrictions were imposed on the movement of people under 22 years and on the eligibility for travel permits of workers with experience in agriculture and turf-cutting. The Irish state negotiated an agreement with its British counterpart in 1941 that controlled, regulated and monitored the flow of emigrants (CONNOLLY, 2000; DELANEY, 2000). In the years following the end of the Second World War in 1945, both Irish and British controls on movement were gradually dismantled. Notwithstanding significant pressure applied to the Fianna Fáil administration in 1947 and the inter-party government in 1948 to restrict the freedom of females under 21 years of age to leave, a ban on emigration was not introduced. Much of the clamour for the enforcement of an age restriction on female emigration was as a result of anxiety on the part of politicians and Catholic clergy about the number of young Irish women travelling to Great Britain (DELANEY, 2000). Since the 1950s the Irish state has not attempted to control or regulate emigration out of the country. In fact from the 1970s onwards, for the first time, the Irish state allocated funding for voluntary advice centres for intending emigrants, and FÁS, the employment and training agency, arranged placements in other European Union countries (NESC; Ó GRÁDA, 1997).

Although all parties resisted pressure for direct prohibition, emigration was a much-debated political issue in independent Ireland in the postwar years. In the general election of February 1948, as TRAVERS (1989) has demonstrated, the failure of Fianna Fáil to reduce the level of emigration was used to underline the inadequacies of the party's economic policy. When the inter-party government took office in 1948 one of its actions was to establish the Commission on Emigration and Other Population Problems, which reported in 1954 (COMMISSION ON EMIGRATION). On publication the report, which contained much sensible analysis and an outline for the development of Irish economic policy, was politely ignored by politicians and civil servants (DELANEY, 2000). Throughout the 1950s emigration frequently emerged in political debates, especially during the March 1957 general election campaign, when the state of the Irish economy was the foremost concern of all parties (DELANEY, 1998). No political party had a stated policy on emigration as such, apart from the putative reduction of the numbers leaving the country by the creation of large-scale employment. Few differences in emphasis or innovative 'solutions' were evident. LEE (1989) has underlined the complacency on the part of the Irish elite and concluded that the 'emigration figures for the forties and fifties stand as a permanent commentary on the collective calibre of the possessing classes'.[29] At the same time, politicians or civil servants could do little else but roundly condemn the 'evils of emigration' on regular occasions. By the 1960s, with the marked reduction in movement out of the country, emigration declined in importance as a political issue, only to re-emerge again in the late 1980s. The upsurge in movement out of the country in the 1980s prompted a major report on the economic and social implications of emigration (NESC).[30]

The Rev. John A. O'Brien and his collaborators in the volume of essays *The Vanishing Irish*, first published in 1953, had little doubt about the impact of mass emigration on twentieth-century Ireland, notwithstanding the awkward complicating factor that the population of independent Ireland had increased slightly between 1946 and 1951. Nevertheless, the alarmist tone that permeated *The Vanishing Irish*, presumably in part derived from the 'burning love of Ireland' which was 'common to all these contributors', was indicative of the widespread contemporary concern about the effects of emigration in the mid-twentieth century (O'BRIEN). What is perhaps most intriguing is that few contemporaries actually dared to outline some of the possible benefits of this outflow of population to other countries, such as the fact that it enabled those who left to enjoy a higher standard of living, and those who stayed behind to have greater access to resources such as land and employment. The Commission on Emigration and Other Population Problems did tentatively underline some of the positive consequences (COMMISSION ON EMIGRATION). But the dominant assumption was that the effects of emigration were uniformly deleterious.

The government of Northern Ireland under devolved rule (1920-72) was not unduly concerned with emigration, mainly because the flow contained a disproportionate number of Catholics, ensuring that the delicate demographic balance of the province, on which so much hinged, was maintained (KENNEDY, 1994). Citizens of Northern Ireland were able to participate in empire migration schemes in the interwar years, and according to FITZPATRICK (1998) leading politicians such as Sir James Craig, first prime minister of Northern Ireland, encouraged empire settlement. The attitude towards empire migration was shaped by a desire to demonstrate in practical terms the full integration of Northern Ireland within imperial schemes and more viscerally by the knowledge that Catholics were more likely to emigrate (FITZPATRICK, 1998; FEDOROWICH, 1999). During the Second World War, the government encouraged the transfer of workers to Great Britain for essential war production and it is estimated that roughly 60,000 people left Northern Ireland for employment 'across the water' (BLAKE). The controls on travel to Great Britain imposed in 1940 also applied to movement from Northern Ireland, because of security concerns relating to the extensive land border between the two Irish states. Naturally this was particularly irksome for travellers from Northern Ireland, who notwithstanding their status as British citizens, were subject to the same restrictions as citizens of a neutral and 'foreign' country. In the postwar period, until the imposition of direct rule from Westminster in 1972, it appears that the state displayed little interest in emigration from Northern Ireland. Since the flow was directed mainly towards Great Britain, and was therefore conceived as the interregional movement of labour within the United Kingdom, it was impolitic to refer to emigration as a 'problem'. In addition, the combination of the over-representation of Catholics in the flow and the consequence that emigration reduced unemployment in Northern Ireland, ensured that this subject exercised few minds at Stormont.

Moving away from the realm of debate and policy, the actual impact of emigration on Irish society after 1921 may be assessed on a number of levels. One of the more obvious consequences has been population decline. Independent Ireland had the unenviable distinction of being the only country in the world to have declined in population more or less continuously between 1845 and 1961 (Ó GRÁDA and WALSH, 1994). In 1926 the population was just under 3 million people; by the early 1960s this had fallen to 2.8 million people, just 43 per cent of the 1841 population (WALSH, 1972). The greatest decreases were recorded from 1911-1926, partly due to the outflow associated with the end of union in 1921, and in the 1950s as a result of mass emigration. Since the rate of natural increase* in independent Ireland rose slightly over time, the absence of sustained population growth from 1921 until the 1950s was a direct consequence of people leaving the country (WALSH, 1989). The 1960s and

1970s marked a watershed in Irish demographic history since for the first time sustained population growth was evident, due to a lower level of emigration, return migration and the steady rate of natural increase*. By the early 1980s the population had reached 3.5 million people. From the mid-1990s onwards, immigration also contributed to the overall gain. By April 2000 the estimated population had risen to nearly 3.8 million people, the highest figure recorded since the census of 1881.[31] The experience in Northern Ireland has been somewhat different with sustained population growth since 1921, even with emigration, although in the 1970s the outflow of population virtually negated the natural increase* (KENNEDY, 1994).

By 1961 only four counties located along the eastern seaboard (Dublin, Kildare, Meath and Louth) had a higher population than was recorded in the census of 1926. The regions that experienced the greatest losses were along the western seaboard and in the north-west. For instance, the population of Co. Leitrim declined by 40 per cent, of Co. Mayo by 29 per cent and of Co. Cavan by 31 per cent between 1926 and 1961 (DRUDY). The counties that suffered sustained population decline were those that were the least urbanised and had a high proportion of the population employed in agriculture, with little manufacturing or industrial employment. From the 1970s onwards, with return migration and a decrease in emigration to other countries, the population of many counties remained relatively stable or recorded slight gains. Nevertheless, internal migration to Dublin together with low rates of natural increase resulted in continuing population decline in some areas such as Leitrim, Roscommon and Cavan (Ó GRÁDA and WALSH, 1994). Rural depopulation was, of course, not unique to twentieth-century Ireland; what was unusual was that the process, universal in the western world, was mainly driven by emigration to other countries, rather than by internal migration. In Northern Ireland, the depopulation of rural areas that had characterised the late nineteenth century was from 1921 onwards more or less confined to remote rural districts, and only two counties along the border, Fermanagh and Tyrone, experienced significant population decline between 1926 and 1971.

The other obvious demographic consequence of emigration was the fact that a substantial number of people born on the island of Ireland lived in other countries after 1921 (see Table 4). For instance in 1931 over 1.6 million people recorded as born in Ireland were living in the United States, Canada, Australia and Great Britain, compared with 4 million living in the 32 counties of Ireland (COMMISSION ON EMIGRATION). In 1991 the number of Irish-born living in the same countries was 1.1 million people, compared with a home population of 5 million people. In Great Britain the Irish-born population in 1991, including those from Northern Ireland, was 837,464 people, or 1.5 per cent of the total population (HICKMAN and WALTER).

Table 4 Population of Ireland (32 counties) and geographical distribution of Irish-born persons, 1921-1991(000s)

	Population of Ireland	United States	Canada	Australia	Britain	Total for countries listed
		Irish-born persons living in:				
1921	4,354[a]	1,037	93	106	524	1,760
1931	4,176[a]	924	108	79	505	1,616
1951	4,331	520	86	48	716	1,370
1961	4,243	406	31[c]	50	951	1,438
1971	4,514	291	38[c]	64	957	1,350
1991	5,127	187[b]	28[c]	77	837	1,129

[a] Estimated.

[b] Includes an estimate for those born in Northern Ireland (on the basis of the 1980 census data).

[c] Data are available only for those born in independent Ireland.

Sources: National Censuses, 1920-1991. Data are for dates proximate to the stated years.

The effects of mass emigration on the labour market in independent Ireland and Northern Ireland are more difficult to identify. There is little doubt, however, that emigration reduced the absolute level of unemployment (and underemployment) for most of the twentieth century, north and south. It was feared that the return of thousands of emigrants to Britain after the Second

World War would exacerbate structural unemployment in both economies (ISLES and CUTHBERT; LEE, 1989). The concern was so acute that the Irish government suggested to the British authorities in 1944 that the return of Irish emigrants be staggered over time (DELANEY, 2000). After the end of the war, the supposed return exodus did not come to pass, mainly because of the acute labour shortage in postwar Great Britain.

Assessing the impact of mass emigration on the development and performance of the two Irish economies since 1921 is a daunting task. In the first instance, the relationship between emigration and economic development is not as straightforward as might be expected. Echoing the earlier views of the Commission on Emigration in 1955, Walsh has argued that, contrary to conventional wisdom, mass emigration from independent Ireland in the 1950s had no long-term impact on economic performance (COMMISSION ON EMIGRATION; WALSH, 1989). So even though the state of the economy was the major determinant of emigration, the inverse relationship was not always evident. Another frequently cited consequence of mass emigration was that it reduced the level of demand for both goods and services produced by Irish manufacturers, thereby inhibiting economic development (MEENAN, 1970). This Keynesian argument, that an expansion of demand within the home market would foster economic growth, ignores the danger that, in the absence of emigration, higher unemployment (and underemployment) would have held down aggregate demand, depressing the average standard of living below the already low levels that prevailed in the 1940s and 1950s. The experience of the 1960s and again of the late 1990s demonstrates that for a small open economy the key to economic growth, and by implication employment creation, is through foreign investment and service to European and world markets (Ó GRÁDA and WALSH, 1994).

The impact of the emigration of professionals, graduates and skilled workers is a complex issue. At first glance, the initial investment involved on the part of Irish taxpayers for the education and training of skilled emigrants is not repaid. However, labour shortages either in Northern Ireland and independent Ireland, have been rare, and usually confined to specific occupations, such as skilled construction workers during the hospital building programme initiated by the inter-party government in the late 1940s, or computer professionals in the 1990s. A second important point relates to the profile of the return flow both in the 1960s and 1970s and, more recently, the late 1990s. It appears that the emigration of Irish skilled workers and professionals is sensitive to economic conditions at home, in that in times of prosperity the return profile contains a high proportion of those with skills, acquired either before leaving or in the receiving country (HUGHES and WALSH, 1976). Interestingly there is also evidence of a 'brain gain'. Of a sample of over 500 returned emigrants interviewed in the mid-1970s, over three quarters had no skill before they left. Yet on return 40 per cent of these unskilled workers had acquired a skill in Great Britain.[32] Similarly, it is likely that the return flow in the late 1990s also contained a significant proportion of skilled migrants, reflecting the opportunities for mobility within the global labour market. In essence, the issue of the costs of 'brain drain' arises only when emigration is a permanent and irreversible move. No such permanence existed in the closely integrated Irish, British, and, by the 1990s, international labour market.

Perhaps one of the more politically unpalatable consequences of emigration since 1921 was the impact on the living standards of those who did not leave Ireland. As MEENAN observed, emigration allowed those who remained at home to enjoy a higher standard of living than would otherwise have been the case. In 1987 a candid (and at the time controversial) admission by a leading politician, Brian Lenihan, that 'after all, we can't all live on a small island',[33] was a recognition of the fact that emigration, by relieving pressure on scarce resources, contributed directly to an increase in living standards for those who stayed behind. This was part of a long-range process from the mid-nineteenth century onwards (see O'ROURKE, 1995). Reduced demand for resources, higher wage levels, especially for scarce, skilled workers, and a lower burden on the exchequer for welfare payments, all ensured that living standards continued to rise over the course of the twentieth century (O'ROURKE, 1994). This was, of course, scant consolation for those who left. In addition, the flow of remittances until the early 1960s increased the income of many households in rural and urban Ireland. In some exceptional cases, such as Co. Mayo in 1960, remittances and pensions constituted 10 per cent of personal income (Ó GRÁDA and WALSH, 1994).

The social consequences of twentieth-century Irish emigration are more elusive. There is little doubt that the exodus of young people created a skewed population profile, with high proportions of young and older age cohorts, leading to a high level of dependency over time (Ó GRÁDA and WALSH, 1994). The economically-active population declined by 11 per cent between 1936 and 1966, whereas the numbers in the dependent age-groups increased by 10 per cent.[34] It has also been suggested that the loss of so many young people, albeit in some cases for a temporary period, resulted in the maintenance of a socially conservative society, with few demands for change (KENNEDY ET AL). On the other hand, it might also be argued that the nature of twentieth-century Irish emigration, with constant movement back and forth across the Irish Sea, frequent contact between emigrants and non-migrants, and large-scale return migration, influenced the pace of socio-cultural change. For instance, it may be further speculated that the campaign for gender equality that developed in independent Ireland in the early 1970s was in part driven by returned female emigrants from Great Britain who were accustomed to a different set of norms in relation to the position, status and remuneration of women.

The personal impact of emigration is only beginning to be explored through the use of oral history to record and chart the experience of movement and settlement outside Ireland after 1921. What emerges from the few published accounts of emigration based on personal testimony is the varied nature of the emigrant experience, conditioned by social class, gender and perceived ethnic identity together with the response to Irish immigration from within the host society (LENNON, MCADAM and O'BRIEN; O'GRADY; SCHWEITZER). Another form of personal testimony is diaries. POOLEY demonstrates how the diary of a young woman from Londonderry who left for London in the 1930s offers a unique insight into the impact of emigration on one individual. Only with further research using oral history, letters and diaries will the complete range of experiences be recovered and the fuller picture of the impact of emigration on individuals become discernible.

It has also been asserted that mass emigration explains the absence of social unrest and sustained class conflict in twentieth-century Ireland (CROTTY; MEENAN). As one contemporary publication declared in 1953: 'if emigration were to be stopped tomorrow conditions favourable to social revolution might easily arise'.[35] This view was frankly articulated in the 1950s by Alexis Fitzgerald in his reservation to the reports of the Commission on Emigration and Other Population Problems. In Fitzgerald's view, emigration released 'social tensions which would otherwise explode'.[36] Naturally this reflects the views and norms of a member of the elite section of Irish society, but the underlying assumption is worth examining. Class conflict was virtually absent in postwar Ireland and it is not unreasonable to argue that one consequence of mass emigration was that it involved the exile of literally hundreds of thousands of unemployed or underemployed young people who in other circumstances may have agitated for social and political change. The contours of the history of twentieth-century Ireland until the 1970s may well have been different in the absence of mass emigration, with greatly increased levels of unemployment and poverty and perhaps even sustained efforts to reconstitute the social structure. Emigration was at once an outlet for the relief of potential class tensions and an avenue for social mobility.

CONCLUSION

Irish emigration up to the 1960s continued the pattern set in earlier decades, in terms of the numbers who left, the lasting consequences for Irish society, and the impact on the migrants themselves. It differed from the pattern of earlier periods in that most emigration was now short distance movement to Great Britain. This growing dominance of Great Britain as a destination reflected both ease of access to the British labour market and the barriers to entry into the United States introduced in the interwar years. Great Britain was just 'across the water' and the resulting sense of proximity was crucial to the whole emigrant experience. Even for those who did travel long distances to North America or Australia, advances in transport technology from the mid-twentieth century allowed for repeated return visits. What mattered was not necessarily the reality of a return, since many twentieth-century emigrants stayed abroad permanently, but the active vision of being able to return home if circumstances so dictated. Emigrants remained highly sensitive to changes in conditions at home, as was seen in the 1970s and late 1990s.

A further element that differed from the nineteenth-century context centres on the issue of responsibility. No longer could politicians in independent Ireland lay the blame for large-scale emigration on the effects of British misrule. The political elite in independent Ireland failed to develop an effective response to the inevitable desire of people to achieve a standard of living above the level of simple survival. It was only in the 1960s, when fundamental changes in economic policy finally resulted in large-scale employment creation, that the imperative to leave lessened. Notwithstanding frequent promises from the lips of Irish politicians to 'eradicate the evil of emigration', the benefits of this movement of people were obvious if rarely stated.

Emigration from twentieth-century Ireland is often viewed as a uniquely Irish phenomenon. In a European context, however, this was far removed from the reality. Portugal, Spain, Greece and Italy were also emigration-prone societies, with large numbers leaving for employment in the advanced economies of western Europe in the 1950s and 1960s (DELANEY, 2000). Within the United Kingdom, Northern Ireland was not the only constituent part to lose a significant share of its population to other regions, as Scotland underwent a similar process. From the mid-nineteenth century until the 1920s the rate of emigration from Ireland was far higher than from most other European countries. By the end of the twentieth century, however, Ireland had moved closer to the European norm in terms of emigration (see appendix). It is also worth noting that Spain, Italy and Portugal, like independent Ireland, became countries of immigration by the 1990s, reversing previous historical patterns. In the twentieth century, emigration was a global phenomenon, impacting on most societies either as sending or receiving states, and shaping the ethnic composition of populations the world over.

Appendix Rates of net migration for the European Union per 1,000 of the average population, 1960-1998

	EU	Belgium	Denmark	Germany	Greece	Spain	France	Ireland*	Italy	Luxembourg	Netherlands	Austria	Portugal	Finland	Sweden	UK
1960-64	0.6	1.5	0.2	2.2	-4.9	-3.5	6.5	-7.4	-1.8	6.5	0.3	0.1	-8.7	-2.5	1.4	1.1
1965-69	-0.1	1.8	0.2	2.9	-4.1	-0.9	1.9	-5.1	-1.8	2.6	0.8	1.4	-19.1	-4.1	3.1	-0.8
1970-74	0.6	0.9	1.3	2.2	-2.8	-0.9	2.2	3.4	-0.8	11.1	2.0	2.5	-5.2	0.3	0.9	-0.6
1975-79	0.8	0.7	0.4	0.2	6.1	0.8	0.6	3.1	0.1	3.9	2.6	-0.4	9.7	-1.5	2.0	-0.2
1980-84	0.2	-0.7	0.2	0.0	1.8	0.0	1.0	-1.9	-0.5	1.1	1.0	0.7	0.5	0.8	0.6	-0.2
1985-89	1.3	0.8	1.2	4.2	2.4	-0.5	0.9	-9.3	0.0	5.9	1.9	2.8	-4.5	0.5	2.9	1.1
1990-94	2.9	1.9	2.0	7.0	5.7	0.4	1.3	-0.4	-1.9	10.5	2.7	7.5	-1.3	1.8	3.7	1.3
1995-98	1.7	1.0	3.3	2.5	2.1	1.1	0.7	4.7	2.1	9.7	1.8	0.6	1.1	0.9	1.0	1.6

* These data refer to independent Ireland only.

Source: Eurostat, Demographic Statistics: Data, 1960-99 (1999).

NOTES

1 John B. Keane, *Self-portrait* (Cork, 1964), p. 32.

2 COURTNEY discusses the issues surrounding the quantification of Irish emigration, with a particular focus on the 1980s and 1990s. For the earlier period, see COMMISSION ON EMIGRATION, pp. 115-20.

3 NESC, tab. 2.5, p. 55.

4 Central Statistics Office, *Population and Migration Estimates [Apr. 1998-Apr. 1999]*, Oct. 1999, p. 1.

5 Ibid.

6 'Statistics of Emigration and Passenger Movement', *Irish Trade Journal and Statistical Bulletin*, June 1951, p. 78.

7 Central Statistics Office, *Population and Migration Estimates [Apr. 1998-Apr. 1999]*, Oct. 1999, p. 1.

8 DALY (1999), p. 7.

9 *Census of Population, 1971: vol. I, Population of District Electoral Divisions, Towns and Larger Units of Area* (Dublin, 1972), xxii.

10 The totals for *net* emigration between 1926 and 1996 are 572,840 for males and 546,470 for females.

11 Estimates of migration from Northern Ireland, 1991-99, supplied by Demography and Methodology Branch, Northern Ireland Statistics and Research Agency.

12 *Commission on Higher Education, 1960-67, Report* (Dublin, 1967), I, Pr. 9389, p. 247.

13 Denis P. Barritt and Charles F. Carter, *The Northern Ireland Problem* (2nd ed., London, 1972), pp. 107-8.

14 GARVEY, p. 25.

15 COMMISSION ON EMIGRATION, p. 134.

16 HANNAN (1972), p. 180.

17 D. A. Gillmor, *Agriculture in the Republic of Ireland* (Budapest, 1977), p. 35.

18 National Archives of Ireland, DT S 16325 B, Emigration to Britain: brief statement of the policy of the government of Ireland, 7 Oct. 1960.

19 Liam Ryan, 'Urban Poverty', in Stanislaus Kennedy (ed.), *One Million Poor?* (Dublin, 1981), p. 35. The report was undertaken in 1944 by a group at University College, Cork, under the direction of the president, Alfred O'Rahilly, and John Busteed, the professor of economics. A final report was never published.

20 Quoted in Kevin Whelan, 'The Famine and Post-Famine Adjustment', in William Nolan (ed.), *The Shaping of Ireland* (Cork, 1986), p. 160.

21 Trinity College Dublin, Marsh Papers, MS 8306, rural survey, s.1, Co. Mayo and Co. Sligo, conducted by J. P. Beddy, n.d. [Oct. 1948], p. 4.

[22] DALY (1981), p. 81.

[23] MC NABB, p. 206.

[24] HANNAN (1973), p. 4.

[25] Trinity College Dublin, Marsh Papers, MS 8306, rural survey, s.4: counties Leitrim and Donegal, n.d. [Sept. 1948], p. 2.

[26] 'Statistics of Emigration and Passenger Movement', *Irish Trade Journal and Statistical Bulletin,* June 1951, p. 76.

[27] O'BRIEN, p. 3.

[28] *Dáil Éireann Debates,* LXV, 17 Feb. 1937, col. 332.

[29] LEE (1989), p. 385.

[30] For an assessment of this report, see Ó CÍNNÉIDE ET AL.

[31] Central Statistics Office, *Population and Migration Estimates [Apr. 1999-Apr. 2000],* Sept. 2000, p. 1.

[32] WHELAN and HUGHES, p. 45. My thanks go to Kevin Dillon of the Library of the Economic and Social Research Institute, Dublin, for locating a copy of this important report for me.

[33] Quoted in MAC LAUGHLIN (1994), p. 40.

[34] Cited in KENNEDY ET AL, p. 147.

[35] Quoted in LEE (1989), p. 374.

[36] COMMISSION ON EMIGRATION, p. 272.

[37] Dudley Baines, *Emigration from Europe 1815-1930* (Cambridge, 1995), table 3, p. 4.

GLOSSARY

COHORT DEPLETION TECHNIQUES: A method by which survivorship ratios are established for a specific age cohort of population by comparing the results of successive censuses, thereby arriving at an estimate of the numbers who emigrated. This measure makes no adjustment for mortality.

GROSS EMIGRATION: The total number of persons who leave with the intention of taking up residence in another country.

INTERNAL MIGRATION: Migration within the boundaries of a state or other political unit, sometimes calculated in the Irish case as inter-county migration.

MIGRANT NETWORKS: Networks based on ties of kinship, friendship and membership of the same community that connect migrants, returned migrants, and non-migrants in both the sending and receiving countries.

NATURAL INCREASE: The excess of births over deaths in a population.

NET EMIGRATION: The difference between gross inflows and gross outflows of population, or in other words, between those leaving and those entering within an intercensal period.

WAGE DIFFERENTIALS: In relation to the study of international migration, this is usually understood as the gap in wage levels between the sending and receiving countries.

SELECT BIBLIOGRAPHY

The sources for the study of Irish emigration after 1921 are diverse and much of the research has been completed by sociologists, geographers and economists rather than historians. As yet, a collection of primary sources dealing with the twentieth century has not been published. For statistical information, the Census of Population for both Northern Ireland and independent Ireland provide the basic data. More detailed statistics for the period prior to 1952 can be found in the Reports of the Commission on Emigration and Other Population Problems, 1948-54 (COMMISSION ON EMIGRATION), and the major report on Irish emigration commissioned by the National Economic and Social Council and published in 1991 (NESC). These reports may be supplemented by the information published annually in the *Statistical Abstract* (independent Ireland) and the *Ulster Year Books* (Northern Ireland). From the 1980s, the Central Statistics Office began to analyse and publish more detailed emigration data based on a number of sources including the Labour Force Surveys: a discussion of the various estimates of emigration can be found in COURTNEY. The importance of assessing the Irish experience in a comparative context has been underlined in this study and the best general account of migration in postwar Europe still remains John Salt and Hugh Clout (eds), *Migration in Postwar Europe* (Oxford 1976).

AKENSON, D. H. *Half the World from Home: Perspectives on the Irish in New Zealand, 1860-1950* (Wellington 1990).

————, *Occasional Papers on the Irish in South Africa* (Grahamstown 1991).

————, *The Irish Diaspora* (Belfast 1993). An important study by the leading historian of the Irish diaspora.

ARENSBERG, Conrad M. and KIMBALL, Solon T. *Family and Community in Ireland* (2nd ed., Cambridge MA 1968).

50

BIELENBERG, Andy (ed.), *The Irish Diaspora* (London 2000). A recent collection of essays that examines aspects of twentieth-century Irish emigration.

BLAKE, John W. *Northern Ireland in the Second World War* (Belfast 1957). Useful on wartime movement to Great Britain.

BOWEN, Kurt. *Protestants in a Catholic State: Ireland's Privileged Minority* (Dublin 1983).

BREEN, Richard, HEATH, Anthony F. and WHELAN, Christopher T. 'Educational Inequality in Ireland, North and South', in HEATH, BREEN and WHELAN (eds), *Ireland North and South*, pp. 187-213.

COLEMAN, D. A. 'Demography and Migration in Ireland, North and South', in HEATH, BREEN and WHELAN (eds), *Ireland North and South*, pp. 69-115. A brief demographic overview.

COMMISSION ON EMIGRATION AND OTHER POPULATION PROBLEMS, *Reports* (Dublin [1955]).

COMPTON, Paul. 'Religious Affiliation and Demographic Variability in Northern Ireland', *Transactions of the Institute of British Geographers*, new ser., 1, no. 4 (1976), pp. 433-52.

————, *Demographic Trends in Northern Ireland* (Northern Ireland Economic Council Report no. 57, Belfast 1986).

————, 'Migration Trends for Northern Ireland: Links with Great Britain', in John Stillwell, Philip Rees and Peter Boden (eds), *Migration Processes and Patterns*, Vol. 2: *Population Redistribution in the United Kingdom* (London 1991), pp. 81-99.

CONNOLLY, Tracey. 'Irish Workers in Britain during the Second World War', in Brian Girvin and Geoffrey Roberts (eds), *Ireland and the Second World War: Politics, Society and Remembrance* (Dublin 2000), pp. 121-32.

————, 'Emigration from Ireland to Britain during the Second World War', in BIELENBERG (ed.), *The Irish Diaspora*, pp. 51-64.

CORCORAN, Mary P. *Irish Illegals: Transients Between Two Societies* (Westport CT 1993).

COURTNEY, Damien. 'A Quantification of Irish Migration with Particular Emphasis on the 1980s and 1990s', in BIELEN-BERG (ed.), *The Irish Diaspora*, pp. 287-316. A thorough discussion of the available statistics for independent Ireland and useful on the background to the preparation of recent emigration estimates.

CROTTY, Raymond D. *Irish Agricultural Production: Its Volume and Structure* (Cork 1966).

DALY, Mary E. 'Women in the Workforce from Pre-Industrial to Modern Times', *Saothar,* 7 (1981), pp. 74-82.

————, *Women and Work in Ireland* (Studies in Irish Economic and Social History no. 7, Dublin 1997). An excellent study, concise but wide-ranging.

————, 'The Irish Family Since the Famine: Continuity and Change', *Irish Journal of Feminist Studies*, 3, no. 2 (1999), pp. 1-21. A detailed analysis of patterns that focuses on the post-1921 period.

DELANEY, Enda. 'State, Politics and Demography: the Case of Irish Emigration, 1921-71', *Irish Political Studies*, 13 (1998), pp. 25-49.

————, 'Placing Postwar Irish Migration to Britain in a Comparative European Perspective, 1945-1981', in BIELEN-BERG (ed), *The Irish Diaspora*, pp. 331-56.

————, *Demography, State and Society: Irish Migration to Britain, 1921-1971* (Liverpool and Montreal/Kingston 2000).

————, 'Gender and Twentieth-Century Irish Migration, 1921-1971', in Pamela Sharpe (ed.), *Women, Gender and Labour Migration: Historical and Global Perspectives* (London 2001), pp. 209-23.

DRUDY, P. J. 'Migration between Ireland and Britain since Independence', in P. J. Drudy (ed.), *Ireland and Britain Since 1922* (Irish Studies 5, Cambridge 1986), pp. 107-23.

DUFFY, Patrick. 'Literary Reflections on Irish Migration in the Nineteenth and Twentieth Centuries', in Russell King, John Connell and Paul White (eds), *Writing Across Worlds: Literature and Migration* (London 1995), pp. 20-38.

FEDOROWICH, Kent. 'The Problems of Disbandment: The Royal Irish Constabulary and Imperial Migration, 1919-29', *Irish Historical Studies*, XXX, no. 117 (1996), pp. 88-110.

————, 'Reconstruction and Resettlement: The Politicization of Irish Migration to Australia and Canada, 1919-29', *English Historical Review*, CXIV, no. 459 (1999), pp. 1143-78.

FITZPATRICK, David. *Irish Emigration, 1801-1921* (Studies in Irish Economic and Social History no. 1, Dublin 1984). An impressive study of nineteenth and early twentieth-century Irish emigration.

————, 'Emigration, 1871-1921', in W. E. Vaughan (ed.), *A New History of Ireland*, Vol. V: *Ireland under the Union, pt. ii (1870-1921)*(Oxford 1996), pp. 606-52.

————, *The Two Irelands, 1912-1939* (Oxford 1998).

FORSYTHE, Frank P. and BOROOAH, Vani K. 'The Nature of Migration between Northern Ireland and Great Britain: A Preliminary Analysis Based on the Labour Force Surveys, 1986-88', *Economic and Social Review*, 23, no. 2 (1992), pp. 105-27.

GARRETT, Paul Michael. 'The Abnormal Flight: The Migration and Repatriation of Irish Unmarried Mothers', *Social History*, 25, no. 3 (2000), pp. 330-43.

GARVEY, Donal. 'The History of Migration Flows in the Republic of Ireland', *Population Trends*, no. 39 (1985), pp. 22-30. Succinct and well-informed account of patterns until the mid-1980s.

GEARY, R. C. and HUGHES, J. G. *Internal Migration in Ireland* (ESRI Paper no. 54, Dublin 1970).

GEMERY, Henry A. 'Immigrants and Emigrants: International Migration and the US Labour Market in the Great Depression', in Timothy J. Hatton and Jeffrey G. Williamson (eds), *Migration and the International Labour Market, 1850-1939* (London 1994), pp. 175-99.

GISH, Oscar. 'Emigration and the Supply and Demand for Medical Manpower: The Irish Case', *Minerva*, 7 (1969), pp. 668-79.

GLYNN, Sean. 'Irish Immigration to Britain, 1911-1951: Patterns and Policy', *Irish Economic and Social History*, VIII (1981), pp. 50-69.

GRIMES, Seamus. 'Postwar Irish Immigration in Australia', in KING (ed.), *Contemporary Irish Migration*, pp. 42-54.

GUDGIN, Graham. 'The Northern Ireland Labour Market', in HEATH, BREEN and WHELAN (eds), *Ireland North and South*, pp. 251-84.

GUINNANE, Timothy W. *The Vanishing Irish: Households, Migration and the Rural Economy in Ireland, 1850-1914* (Princeton NJ 1997).

HANLON, Gerard. 'The Emigration of Irish Accountants: Economic Restructuring and Producer Services in the Periphery', *Irish Journal of Sociology*, 1 (1991), pp. 52-65.

————, 'Technical Experience or Social Myth: Ireland and the International Professional Labour Market', in MAC LAUGHLIN (ed.), *Location and Dislocation in Contemporary Irish Society*, pp. 323-39.

HANNAN, Damian F. 'Migration Motives and Migration Differentials among Irish Rural Youth', *Sociologia Ruralis*, IX (1969), pp. 195-219.

————, *Rural Exodus: A Study of the Forces Influencing the Large-Scale Migration of Irish Rural Youth* (London 1970). A seminal study of migration from Co. Cavan in the 1960s.

————, 'Kinship, Neighbourhood and Social Change in Irish Rural Communities', *Economic and Social Review*, 3, no. 2 (1972), pp. 163-88.

————, 'Irish Emigration Since the War' (unpublished RTE Thomas Davis Lecture, 1973).

————, *Displacement and Development: Class, Kinship and Social Change in Irish Rural Communities* (ESRI Paper no. 96, Dublin 1979).

————, 'Peasant Models and the Understanding of Social and Cultural Change in Rural Ireland', in P. J. Drudy (ed.), *Ireland: Land, Politics and People* (Irish Studies 2, Cambridge 1982), pp. 141-65.

HART, Peter. 'The Protestant Experience of Revolution in Southern Ireland', in Richard English and Graham Walker (eds), *Unionism in Modern Ireland* (Dublin 1996), pp. 81-98. Good on the reasons underlying the Protestant emigrant flow in the early 1920s.

————, *The I.R.A. and its Enemies: Violence and Community in Cork, 1916-1923* (Oxford 1998). Contains a fascinating analysis of the relationship between sectarian violence and Protestant emigration.

HEATH, Anthony F, BREEN, Richard and WHELAN, Christopher T. (eds), *Ireland North and South: Perspectives from Social Science* (Oxford 1999).

HICKMAN, Mary and WALTER, Bronwen. *Discrimination and the Irish Community in Britain* (London 1997).

HUGHES, J. G. *Estimates of Annual Net Migration and their Relationship with Series on Annual Net Passenger Movement: Ireland, 1926-76* (ESRI Memorandum Series no. 122, Dublin 1977). A detailed reconstruction of migration estimates.

————, and WALSH, Brendan M. 'Migration Flows between Ireland, the United Kingdom and the Rest of the World, 1966-71', *European Demographic Information Bulletin*, VII (1976), pp. 125-49.

————, and WALSH, Brendan M. *Internal Migration Flows in Ireland and their Determinants* (ESRI Paper no. 98, Dublin 1980).

ISLES, K. S. and CUTHBERT, Norman. *An Economic Survey of Northern Ireland* (Belfast 1957). Contains a good discussion of emigration patterns from Northern Ireland.

JACKSON, John Archer. *The Irish in Britain* (London 1963).

JOHNSON, David. *The Interwar Economy in Ireland* (Studies in Irish Economic and Social History no. 4, Dublin 1985).

KENNEDY, Kieran A., GIBLIN, Thomas and McHUGH, Deirdre. *The Economic Development of Ireland in the Twentieth Century* (London 1988). Interesting analysis of the place of emigration in Irish economic development.

KENNEDY, Liam. 'Farm Succession in Modern Ireland: Elements of a Theory of Inheritance', *Economic History Review*, XLIV, no. 3 (1991), pp. 477-99.

————, *People and Population change: A Comparative Study of Population Change in Northern Ireland and the Irish Republic* (Dublin and Belfast 1994). Concise and clear account dealing with independent Ireland and Northern Ireland.

KENNEDY, Robert E. Jr. *The Irish: Emigration, Marriage and Fertility* (Berkeley 1973). A seminal study of Irish demographic patterns.

KING, Russell (ed.). *Contemporary Irish Migration* (GSI Special Publications no. 6, Dublin 1991). Useful on the 1980s.

LEE, J.J. 'Continuity and Change in Ireland, 1945-70', in J. J. Lee (ed.), *Ireland, 1945-70* (Dublin 1979), pp. 166-77.

————, *Ireland, 1912-1985: Politics and Society* (Cambridge 1989). Incorporates a thought-provoking and original analysis of post-1921 Irish emigration.

LENNON, Mary, MCADAM, Marie and O'BRIEN, Joanne. *Across the Water: Irish Women's Lives in Britain* (London 1988). A useful collection based on interviews with Irish female emigrants.

LOBO, A. P. and SALVO, J. J. 'Resurgent Irish Immigration to the US in the 1980s and Early 1990s: A Socio-Demographic Profile', *International Migration*, 36, no. 2 (1998), pp. 257-80.

LYNN, Richard. *The Irish Brain Drain* (ESRI Paper no. 43, Dublin 1968).

MAC AMHLAIGH, Donall. *An Irish Navvy: The Diary of an Exile*, trans. from the Irish by Valentin Iremonger (London 1964).

MACLAUGHLIN, Jim (ed.). *Location and Dislocation in Contemporary Irish Society: Emigration and Irish Identities* (Cork 1997).

————, *Ireland: The Emigrant Nursery and the World Economy* (Cork 1994). Provocative if not entirely convincing analysis.

MASSEY, Douglas, ALARCÓN, Rafael, DURAND, Jorge, GONZÁLEZ, Humberto. *Return to Aztlan: The Social Process of International Migration from Western Mexico* (Berkeley CA 1987).

MCCOURT, Frank. *Angela's Ashes* (London 1996).

MCNABB, Patrick. 'Demography' and 'Social Structure', in NEWMAN (ed.), *The Limerick Rural Survey*, pp. 158-92, 193-247.

MCVEIGH, Ann. 'Australia for Ten Pounds', *History Ireland*, 1, no. 3 (1993), pp. 44-46.

MEENAN, James. *The Irish Economy Since 1922* (Liverpool 1970).

MOGEY, John M. *Rural Life in Northern Ireland: Five Regional Studies* (Oxford 1947).

NESC. *The Economic and Social Implications of Emigration* (NESC Report no. 90, Dublin 1991).

NEWMAN, Jeremiah (ed.), *The Limerick Rural Survey, 1958-1964* (Tipperary 1964).

NÍ LAOIRE, Caitríona. 'Conceptualising Irish Rural Youth Migration: A Biographical Approach', *International Journal of Population Geography*, 6 (2000), pp. 229-43.

O'BRIEN, John A. (ed.), *The Vanishing Irish: The Enigma of the Modern World* (New York 1953). Alarmist in tone, but nevertheless a revealing indication of contemporary views.

Ó CINNÉIDE, Séamus, JACKSON, John, STRACHAN, Alan, BOYLAN, Thomas. 'Review Symposium: *The Economic and Social Implications of Emigration*', *Irish Journal of Sociology*, 1 (1991), pp. 66-82.

Ó GRÁDA, Cormac. 'Primogeniture and Ultimogeniture in Rural Ireland', *Journal of Interdisciplinary History*, 10, no. 3 (1980), pp. 491-97.

————, *Ireland: A New Economic History, 1780-1939* (Oxford 1994).

————, *A Rocky Road: The Irish Economy Since the 1920s* (Manchester 1997).

————, and WALSH, Brendan M. 'The Economic Effects of Emigration: Ireland', in Beth J. Asch (ed.), *Emigration and its Effects on the Sending Country* (Santa Monica CA 1994), pp. 97-152. Valuable analysis by an economic historian and an economist.

————, and WALSH, Brendan M. 'Fertility and Population in Ireland, North and South', *Population Studies*, 49, no. 2 (1995), pp. 259-79. Good treatment of the relationship between emigration and religion in independent Ireland and Northern Ireland.

O'GRADY, Anne. *Irish Migration to London in the 1940s and 1950s* (London 1988).

301.412

Irish Women
Irish Migration 63
ed by
Patrick
O'
Sullivan

SELECT BIBLIOGRAPHY

Ó RIAIN, Mícheál. 'Cross-Channel Passenger Traffic, 1960-1990', *Journal of the Statistical and Social Inquiry Society of Ireland*, XXVI (1991-92), pp. 45-90.

O'ROURKE, Kevin. 'Did Labour Flow Uphill? International Migration and Wage Rates in Twentieth-Century Ireland', in George Grantham and Mary MacKinnon (eds), *Labour Market Evolution: The Economic History of Market Integration, Wage Flexibility and the Employment Relation* (London 1994), pp. 139-60.

————, 'Emigration and Living Standards in Ireland Since the Famine', *Journal of Population Economics*, 8 (1995), pp. 407-21. A long-range overview.

POOLEY, Colin. 'From Londonderry to London: Identity and Sense of Place for a Protestant Northern Irish Woman in the 1930s', *Immigrants and Minorities*, 18, nos. 2/3 (1999), pp. 189-213.

ROSE, A. J. 'Irish Migration to Australia in the Twentieth Century', *Irish Geography*, IV (1959), pp. 79-84.

SCHWEITZER, Pam (ed.). *Across the Irish Sea* (2nd ed., London 1991). A collection of interviews with Irish emigrants in Great Britain.

SCULLY, John J. *Agriculture in the West of Ireland: A Study of the Low Farm Income Problem* (Dublin 1971).

SEXTON, J. J. and O'LEARY, Richard. 'Factors Affecting Population Decline in Minority Religious Communities in the Republic of Ireland', in *Building Trust in Ireland: Studies Commissioned by the Forum for Peace and Reconciliation* (Belfast 1996), pp. 255-332. Contains a useful discussion of emigration patterns.

SHUTTLEWORTH, Ian. 'Graduate Emigration from Ireland: A Symptom of Peripherality?', in KING (ed.), *Contemporary Irish Migration*, pp. 83-95.

————, 'Graduate Emigrants: a "New Wave" in Irish Emigration?', in MACLAUGHLIN, (ed.), *Location and Dislocation in Contemporary Irish Society*, pp. 304-22.

TRAVERS, Pauric. '"The Dream Gone Bust": Irish Responses to Emigration, 1922-60', in Oliver MacDonagh and W. F. Mandle (eds), *Irish-Australian Studies* (Canberra 1989), pp. 318-42.

————, '"There Was Nothing For Me There": Irish Female Migration, 1922-71', in Patrick O'Sullivan (ed.), *Irish Women and Irish Migration* (vol. 4 of *The Irish Worldwide: History, Heritage, Identity*) (London 1995), pp. 146-67. An interesting overview of female emigration.

WALSH, Brendan M. *Some Irish Population Problems Reconsidered* (ESRI Paper no. 42, Dublin 1968).

————, 'Influences on Mobility and Employment in Irish Family Farming', *Irish Journal of Agricultural Economics and Rural Sociology*, 2, no. 1 (1969), pp. 13-24.

————, *Migration to the United Kingdom from Ireland, 1961-66* (ESRI Memorandum Series no. 70, Dublin 1970)

————, *Religion and Demographic Behaviour in Ireland* (ERSI Paper no. 55, Dublin 1970).

————, 'Economic and Demographic Adjustment of the Irish Agricultural Labour Force, 1961-66', *Irish Journal of Agricultural Economics and Rural Sociology*, 3, no. 2 (1971), pp. 113-24.

————, 'Postwar Demographic Developments in the Republic of Ireland', *Social Studies*, 1 (1972), pp. 309-17.

————, 'Expectations, Information and Human Migration: Specifying an Econometric Model of Irish Migration to Britain', *Journal of Regional Science*, 14, no. 1 (1974), pp. 107-20.

————, 'Trends in the Religious Composition of the Population in the Republic of Ireland, 1946-71', *Economic and Social Review*, 6, no. 4 (1975), pp. 543-55.

————, *Ireland's Changing Demographic Structure* (Dublin 1989).

————, *Wage Convergence and Integrated Labour Markets: Ireland and Britain, 1841-1991*(Centre for Economic Research, Working Paper 94/6, Dublin 1994).

WALSH, James A. 'Immigration to the Republic of Ireland', *Irish Geography*, 12 (1979), 104-10.

WALTER, Bronwen. *Gender and Irish Migration to Britain* (Anglia Geography Working Paper no. 4, Cambridge 1989).

————, 'Gender and Recent Irish Migration to Britain', in KING (ed.), *Contemporary Irish Migration*, pp. 11-20.

WHELAN, B. J. and HUGHES, J. G. *A Survey of Returned and Intending Emigrants in Ireland* (Dublin 1976).